the facts about
FLOWERING PLANTS

Rebecca Hunter

FRANKLIN WATTS
LONDON · SYDNEY

© Franklin Watts 2003

First published in 2003 by
Franklin Watts
96 Leonard Street
London
EC2A 4XD

Franklin Watts Australia
45-51 Huntley Street
Alexandria
NSW 2015

ISBN: 0-7496-4877-5

A CIP catalogue record for this book is available from
the British Library

Manufactured in China
Planning and production by Discovery Books Limited
Editor: Rebecca Hunter
Design: Keith Williams
Consultant: Jeremy Bloomfield
Illustrations: Peter Bull: page 4, page 9, page 13, page 14.

Photographs:
Bruce Coleman Collection: page 4, 8 (Tore Hagman), 9
(Hans Reinhard), 10 bottom (Joy Langsbury), 11 (Jeff Foott),
15 top (Jules Cowan), 18 top (Joe McDonald), bottom left
(Kim Taylor), 21 top (Jane Burton), 25 top right (Jane Burton);
Discovery Picture Library: page 6 all, 10 top, 20, 22;
Oxford Scientific Films: page 7, 12 (Breck P Kent), 13
bottom (Bob Gibbons), 14, 16 (Richard Packwood), 17
bottom, 18 bottom right (Bert & Babs Wells), 19 (Bob
Gibbons), 21 bottom (Harold Taylor), 23 top (Martyn
Chillmaid), 23 bottom, 24 (Stan Osolinski), 25 bottom
(Carlos Sanches Alonso), 26, 27 (Deni Brown), 28 top, 28
bottom (Max Gibbs), 29 (Mark Hamblin); Photodisc: cover,
page 5, 13 top, 15 bottom, 17 top, 25 top left.

the facts about
FLOWERING PLANTS

Contents

Words in **bold** appear in the glossary on page 30.

Flowering plants

We live in a world that is full of plants. The largest group of plants are those that produce flowers.

The plant kingdom is made up of two groups of plants: those that produce flowers and those that do not. Most plants belong in the group of flowering plants.

Non-flowering plants

Non-flowering plants include mosses, lichens and ferns. These are small, low-growing plants that have no root systems or flowers. They produce spores instead of seeds. **Coniferous** trees such as pines, cedars and firs, produce cones instead of flowers. The seeds grow inside the cones.

▼ Trees are flowering plants. This apple tree in full blossom stands in a field of dandelions.

Flowering plants

When you imagine flowering plants you probably think first of all about the brightly-coloured flowers that grow in gardens and parks or wild in the fields. However flowering plants form a very large group and include many **species** that you may not have thought of.

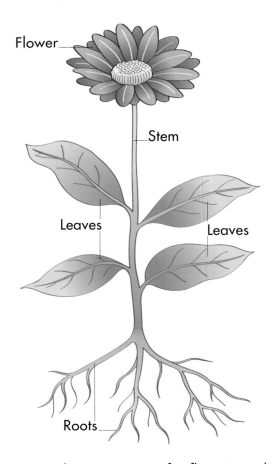

Flower

Stem

Leaves

Leaves

Roots

▲ The main parts of a flowering plant.

All broad-leaved trees are flowering plants. They include, for example, oak trees, beech trees, willows and many other trees. They are known as broad-leaved trees because their leaves are broad and flat, unlike the sharp needles on coniferous trees.

Other flowering plants include fruit trees, vegetables, herbs and grasses. Many grasses such as wheat, barley and sweetcorn are grown for food.

We all love looking at the bright colours and smelling the pleasant scents of flowers, but plants do not produce flowers for our pleasure. Flowers have a very important role ensuring that the next generation of plants will grow.

▲ A meadow full of flowering plants, with non-flowering conifers in the background.

key facts

- The plant kingdom is divided into flowering and non-flowering plants.

- There are more types of flowering plant than non-flowering plant.

- Flowering plants include broad-leaved trees, grasses, vegetables, weeds and herbs.

Seeds

Nearly all flowering plants develop from seeds. Each seed contains an embryo, the young plant, and a store of food to help the embryo develop.

Fruits and nuts

Seeds grow inside the part of a plant called a fruit. We can identify the seeds of edible fruit quite easily. Think of the pips inside a lemon or the stone inside a cherry. Some foods that we call vegetables, like tomatoes and cucumbers, should really be called fruits because they

◄▲ The seeds of a tomato or lemon are inside the fruit. The strawberry's seeds are on the outside.

contain seeds. Beans and peas belong to a group called legumes. Legumes produce their seeds inside a long casing called a pod.

A nut is a seed that is covered in a dry, hard-cased fruit. Acorns, hazelnuts, walnuts and coconuts are all really the seeds of their trees.

◄ These nuts are the fruit of the hazel tree.

See how seeds germinate by growing broad beans. Line the sides of a jar with blotting paper. Put a few broad beans between the paper and the glass. Add a little water and leave the jar somewhere warm for a week. When the beans have germinated, move the jar to somewhere light and watch the bean plants grow.

Germination

Seeds need three things to germinate, or start growing: water, air and warmth. If all three are present the seed can grow. Seeds do not need light to germinate.

To germinate most seeds must be covered with a thin layer of soil. The first stage of germination is when the outer coating of the seed cracks and a tiny root grows downwards into the soil. Next, a tiny shoot develops and grows upwards. Once the shoot reaches the surface of the soil, leaves will start to appear. From then on the plant will need light to grow.

key facts

- Most flowering plants grow from seeds.
- Seeds need air, water and warmth to germinate.
- Seeds do not need light to germinate.

The growing plant

Growing plants get their energy from sunlight. This process is called **photosynthesis**.

Photosynthesis

Photosynthesis is a long word but it can be split up into 'photo', which means light, and 'synthesis', which means making something. So photosynthesis actually means using light to make food. Green plants have a substance in them called **chlorophyll**. Chlorophyll is able to capture the energy in sunlight.

You can do it...

Find out the best conditions for growing seedlings. Put three seedlings in three separate pots. Place one in a dark place, like a cupboard, and put the other two on a sunny windowsill. Water the one in the cupboard and only one of the plants on the windowsill regularly. Which seedling grows best?

As well as sunlight, plants need water and the gas carbon dioxide for photosynthesis to happen. Water is taken in from the soil by the plant's roots and is then passed up the stem to the leaves. The plant's leaves absorb carbon dioxide from the air.

The process of photosynthesis creates glucose, a type of sugar, which the plant uses to develop and grow. It also produces the gas oxygen, which is released back into the air.

◀ Green leaves contain a substance called chlorophyll, which is able to turn the energy in sunlight into food for the plant.

Carbon dioxide is taken in from the air through tiny holes called **stomata**.

Light energy comes from the Sun.

Oxygen is given off into the air through the stomata.

Water is taken in from the soil through the roots.

▲ The process of photosynthesis in a green plant.

▲ Flowering plants have leaves of many different shapes and sizes, but their purpose is the same – to carry out photosynthesis.

key facts

- Photosynthesis is the process by which plants make food from sunlight.

- Green leaves contain chlorophyll which enables photosynthesis to take place.

- Plants need light, water and carbon dioxide to photosynthesize.

Stems and roots

Flowering plants are held up by their stems. Below ground, roots anchor the plants in place and absorb water and **minerals**.

Stems

The stem of a plant is above ground. It has three functions. First, it supports the leaves and flowers. The leaves need to be held out so that they can face the light. The second function of the stem is to carry water and **nutrients** to the leaves, flowers and fruits of the plant. The water is carried in small channels called veins. Thirdly the stem carries the glucose made by photosynthesis (see page 8) from the leaves to the rest of plant.

Some stems are green and flexible; some, such as those in shrubs and trees, are woody and give extra support. The stem of a tree is called the trunk and in large trees can be several metres wide.

◀ The stems of the field poppy are green and flexible. This allows the plant to move in the wind without breaking.

Roots

The roots of a plant are usually below the ground. Roots have two important uses. One is to anchor the plant in the ground and stop it from falling over. The other is to collect water. Large roots divide into small rootlets which are covered with tiny root hairs. These root hairs collect water and pass it up through the roots and stem to the leaves. The water contains minerals and nutrients which the plant needs to grow healthily.

You can do it...

See how water travels through the veins in a plant's stem. Put some celery stalks into a jar containing water that has been coloured with ink or with food colouring. After a few hours you will see the celery change colour. If you cut across a celery stalk, you will see where the veins are in the stalk.

key facts

- Stems support the plant and carry water and minerals to the leaves.

- Roots anchor the plant and absorb water and minerals from the ground.

▶ Mangrove trees grow in thick, sticky mud. Their roots stick up above the mud so that they can absorb the oxygen they need to grow.

Leaves

Leaves come in many shapes and sizes but their main function is the same: to carry out photosynthesis and make food for the plant.

Leaves are a plant's factory, where the production of food takes place. Throughout the hours of daylight, the leaves are making sugars to feed the whole plant, and provide it with the energy it needs to grow.

Structure of a leaf

Most leaves are flat and thin and designed to catch as much sunlight as possible. Simple leaves have just one leaf blade and a leaf stalk. Compound leaves are made up of several leaflets growing out from a leaf stalk.

In a simple leaf there is one large vein called the midrib, which branches out into smaller veins covering the entire leaf.

▲ A compound leaf is made up of several small leaflets growing off the main leaf stalk.

▼ A cross-section of a typical leaf.

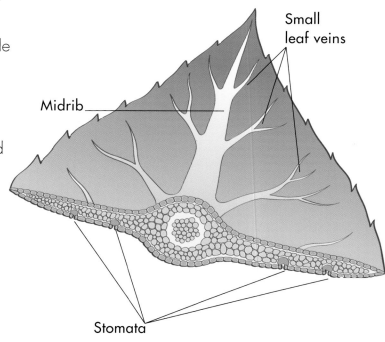

Small leaf veins

Midrib

Stomata

These veins carry water and minerals to the leaf and take away the sugars made by photosynthesis. On the underside of the leaf are many tiny holes called stomata. Gases pass in and out of the leaf through the stomata. The water which has moved through the plant's root and leaf system is also passed out through the stomata as **water vapour**.

You can do it...

Find out for yourself that plants give off water vapour. You will need a fairly small, leafy house plant. Cover the plant with a clear plastic bag and tie it loosely around the stem. Leave the plant in a sunny place for a few hours. When you return you should be able to see tiny water droplets in the bag. They have been released by the plant.

▲ In autumn, leaves on **deciduous** trees die and turn red, yellow and gold. The tree then becomes **dormant** for the winter.

Special features of leaves

Some plants have developed leaves with special features to suit the conditions in which they grow. On mountains, furry leaves keep out the strong sunlight. Plants that live in areas of heavy rain have to protect themselves from getting water-logged. One way they do this is to have waxy leaves, with grooves which channel the water quickly off the leaf.

key facts

- ⬭ Photosynthesis is carried out in the leaves of a plant.

- ⬭ Leaves take in and pass out gases through holes called stomata.

- ⬭ Leaves die and fall off deciduous trees in autumn.

◄ Plants that grow in still or slow-moving water sometimes have wide leaves that float on the surface. The Amazon water-lily produces huge leaves that can be as much as 2 metres in diameter.

Flowers

Flowers come in many beautiful shapes and colours. Their purpose, however, is to produce the seeds that will one day grow into new plants.

The first flowers appeared on Earth about 100 million years ago. Now there are more than 250,000 species of flowering plants. Their flowers range from complex examples such as orchids and lilies to the simple **catkins** of some trees.

The structure of a flower

A flower is made up of several layers. A flower bud is covered with a layer of green sepals, which protect it. When the flower opens it reveals petals, which are usually brightly coloured and may have other markings. In the centre are the male and female parts the flower needs in order to make seeds.

▼ **The parts of a flower.**

Style

Stamen

Stigma

Anther containing pollen

Petal

Ovary

Egg cells

Sepal

You can do it...

Look at a flower and see if you can identify all the parts shown above. Different flowers may have different numbers of petals, anthers and stigmas, but you should be able to see them clearly.

◄ The catkin of the great sallow tree. The stamens are tipped with yellow pollen.

Male and female

The male stamens are long stalks, which carry a sac of pollen at the end called an anther. The female part, the ovary, is at the base of the flower, with the style and stigma above it. The male cells are in the pollen, the female egg cells in the ovary. To make a seed the male and female cells need to join together.

▲ The lily is one of the most colourful of all flowers. It also has a beautiful scent.

▼ The flower heads of some plants, such as this daisy, are made up of small flowers called florets. In a daisy, one 'head' of a flower can be made up of hundreds of florets. Each floret behaves like a flower and produces one seed.

key facts

- Flowers are the reproductive parts of a plant.

- Flowers carry male cells in the pollen and female cells in the ovary.

- Male and female cells join together to make seeds.

Pollination

Pollination happens when the male cells in the pollen are carried to the female parts of another plant.

To produce a seed, the male cells in the pollen must **fertilize** a female egg in the ovary. It is usually better if a flower is not fertilized by its own pollen, so the pollen has to be carried from the anthers of one plant to the stigma of another. Some flowering plants are pollinated by wind, others rely on water or animals.

Wind pollination

Wind-pollinated plants produce a huge amount of pollen. Each catkin, or flower, on a birch tree can contain 5.5 million pollen grains. A single tree may have several thousand catkins. Imagine how much pollen is produced by all the birch trees in a wood! They need to produce so much pollen because only a very small proportion of it will actually find the female parts of another birch tree.

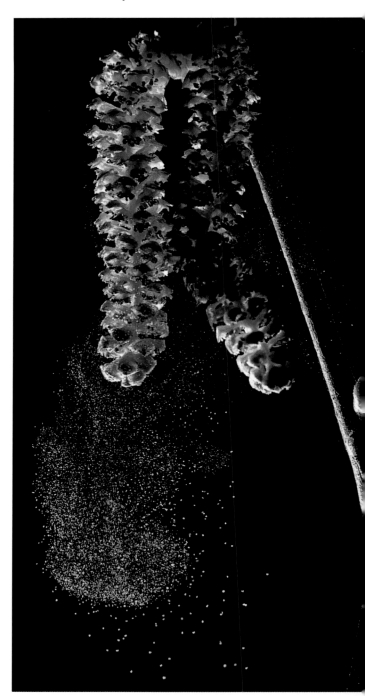

▶ A hazel catkin in the process of shedding its pollen to be carried off by the wind. The flowers on wind-pollinated plants are often in dull colours; they do not need to attract insects to pollinate them.

◄ Wind-pollinated plants such as grasses and trees grow together in large numbers to increase the chances of their pollen reaching another plant.

key facts

- Pollination happens when pollen from the male part of one plant is carried to the female part of another plant.
- Some flowers are pollinated by wind or water.
- Wind-pollinated plants produce an enormous quantity of pollen.

Pollen grains that are carried by the wind need to travel long distances, so they are very small and light. They have a smooth surface and easily drift along on the breeze. The wind can take the grains up as high as 6,000 metres and carry them more than 3,200 kilometres from the parent plants.

Water pollination

Some plants are pollinated by water, and the pollen is dispersed downstream by rivers or streams. The Elodea, or Canadian pondweed, has stamens that grow under-water and release pollen which floats to the surface. The female flower (right) grows on the surface of the water and collects the pollen as it floats by.

Animal pollination

A flower's bright colour, delicious scent and the food it offers attract many animals, especially insects.

An animal visiting the flower may accidentally pick up some pollen on its body. When it then visits another flower of the same species, some of the pollen may rub off on to that flower's stigma. The plant has used the animal to help pollination take place.

◄ The most specialized of all nectar-feeding birds are the South American hummingbirds.

Nectar

Bees and other insects eat pollen, but some plants also produce another food, nectar, to attract pollinators. Nectar is sugary liquid that many animals seem to enjoy. In Africa, sunbirds, sugar birds and honey-eaters are nectar-feeders and eat almost nothing else. They are all so small that they can perch on the flower itself.

◄ A painted lady butterfly feeds on the nectar from a thistle.

▲ The tiny Australian honey possum lives entirely on nectar and pollen. It feeds with a long tongue that reaches deep into flowers. Its fur becomes covered with pollen, which rubs off on the next flower it visits.

◀ The lines that guide insects to the nectar are clearly visible on this mountain pansy.

Scents

Most scents produced by flowers are attractive to insects and people alike. We use flowers such as lily of the valley, lavender and rose to make perfumes and soaps. However, a few flowering plants have particularly nasty smells. The effect is the same: insects are attracted to them and pollination is successful.

key facts

- Flowers can be pollinated by insects, birds, bats, possums and lizards.

- Animals are attracted to flowers by their colour, their scents, and the food they provide.

- Some petals have markings which guide pollinators to the right part of the flower.

Patterns

The spectacular colours of flowers are designed to attract insects. Some are also patterned in a way that guides the insects straight to where the plant wants them. Foxgloves, irises and pansies, for example, have guidelines that lead from the outer edge of the petal down to the centre of the flower. These marks are not unlike the guidelines we use on runways for landing aeroplanes. The insects follow them to reach the nectar. Some insects can actually see ultra-violet markings on flowers that are invisible to us.

From pollen to seed

When a grain of pollen lands on the stigma of another plant this is the first stage in the process of making a seed.

The next stage is that a pollen tube grows out of the pollen grain, down the style and into the ovary. Male sex cells travel down the pollen tube and join with female sex cells, the eggs in the ovary. This is called fertilization, when seeds are formed. After fertilization the ovary gets bigger and turns into the fruit. The fruit's job is to protect the seeds and allow them to ripen.

Dispersing the seeds

When seeds are ripe, the plant needs to get them as far away as possible from itself, to allow them to grow into healthy new plants. Young trees, for example, would not grow well in the shade of a fully-grown tree.

▲ These are the wind-dispersed seeds of the sycamore tree.

Wind dispersal

Some trees produce seeds with wings that allow them to fly far away from the parent plant. The seeds of European maples and sycamores, for example, are like tiny helicopters which can travel long distances across the countryside.

The seeds of the poppy (a flower) are dispersed by the wind in a different way. As the wind blows, the seeds are shaken out of the dry hollow fruit, like pepper out of a pepper pot. The seeds are small and light so they are carried easily by the wind.

You can do it...

Collect as many different types of seed as you can. Can you tell which ones are dispersed by wind and which ones by animals?

▲ The dandelion is an example of a flower that uses wind to disperse its seeds.

Animal dispersal

Fruits have bright colours and smells, and many of them taste good. This makes them attractive to hungry birds and animals. The seeds in a fruit are not digested by the animals and are passed out in their droppings. In this way, the animal has helped to move the seeds away from the parent plant.

Some seeds are covered in tiny hooks. These catch on to the fur of a passing animal so the seed is carried elsewhere.

Water dispersal

The coconut (below) is a seed that is dispersed by water. It has a massive store of food which will last it for a year. This allows the young coconut plant to survive on beaches where there is little fresh water. In this way coconut trees can spread from one **tropical** island to another.

key facts

○ Fertilization is when a male sex cell from a pollen grain joins with a female sex cell in the ovary of a plant.

○ The fruit protects the seeds.

○ Seeds can be dispersed by water, wind or animals.

Life cycle of a sunflower

The easiest way to understand the stages in the life of a flowering plant is to follow its life cycle, starting with a seed.

Sunflowers are annual plants. This means they grow from seed each year. The seeds are large and striped. The first stage of growth is when the seed germinates and sends a rootlet down into the soil and a green shoot upwards.

Sunflower plants grow quickly, at the rate of about 1 cm a day. Most of the growth is concentrated in the tip of the shoot. Sunflower stems are strong because they have to to support a tall plant.

The sunflower's first leaves are called seed leaves. They contain a food store for the plant until the true leaves take over.

The growing plant
The leaves open out flat and wide to catch the Sun. Once established, the energy produced by the leaves is put into growing flowers. At first the flower buds are protected by sturdy green sepals.

You can do it...

Grow your own sunflowers. Plant some sunflower seeds, and identify the stages of the life cycle as they grow.

▼ Stages in the growth of a sunflower seed. The shoot breaks through the soil and sheds its seed covering. The young plant then grows towards the light.

Pollination

The bright yellow petals of the sunflower, and the nectar it produces, attract various insects. These crawl all over the sunflower's face, moving pollen from one floret to another. In this way the flowers are pollinated and seed growth is started. A sunflower head contains hundreds of seeds. Each one can grow another sunflower the following year.

▲ A bee crawls across the face of a sunflower, carrying pollen from one floret to another.

▼ Sunflower seeds are a valuable source of oil. Farmers grow sunflowers so that they can harvest the seeds. The seeds are crushed to remove the oil, which is used in cooking.

key facts

○ Sunflowers are annual plants; they grow from seed each year.

○ The flower of a sunflower is made up of many tiny florets.

○ Sunflower seeds contain a useful cooking oil.

Special adaptations

Plants are found on every continent in the world and have developed a range of **adaptations** to cope with almost all conditions.

Saving water

About 10,000 species (types) of flowering plants are succulents. These plants live in very dry places and have developed a different structure to other plants. Euphorbias and cacti store water in their fleshy stems. Their roots absorb water rapidly and their stems can expand quickly when water is available.

Succulents have no leaves, which minimizes water loss. Their stems are adapted to do the job of photosynthesis.

Avoiding predators

Plants cannot move away from animals that might eat them, so they have developed several forms of protection. Some plants are covered with spines or thorns to deter browsing animals. Others, like the stinging nettle, are protected by fine hairs that sting.

Some plants contain a poison that discourages animals from eating them. Young bracken leaves are filled with the poison cyanide. When the leaves are older, not only are they too tough for most animals to eat, but they contain poisons that can cause blindness and **cancer** in mammals.

◄ The spiny stems of this euphorbia store water. The spines protect the plant from being eaten.

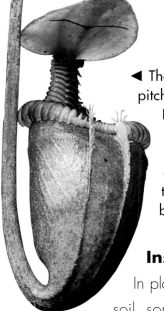

◀ The jug-shaped leaves of the pitcher plant contain liquid. Insects attracted by its smell fall into the liquid and drown. They are digested and the nutrients they contain are absorbed by the plant.

Insect-eating plants

In places with poor-quality soil, some plants get extra nutrients by trapping insects with their leaves. The pitcher plant has special leaves that grow into jug-like pitchers. These contain water and **digestive juices**. If an insect falls into the pitcher it drowns, and is then digested and absorbed by the plant over a period of several days.

Parasitic plants

About one per cent of all flowering plants are parasitic. This means they steal some of their food from other plants. The plants they live on are called hosts. Mistletoe is a parasitic plant that grows on trees.

▶ The Venus flytrap has hinged leaves which snap shut on any insect that lands on them. It takes between 8 and 20 days for a Venus flytrap to digest an insect.

key facts

- Plants can protect themselves from predators with spines, stings and poison.

- Some plants can trap animals and gain extra nourishment from them.

- A small proportion of flowering plants are parasitic.

◀ The sticky white berries of mistletoe are eaten by birds. As the birds wipe their beaks on the bark, the seeds are spread to other tree trunks.

Unusual flowers

Most flowers are fairly small, with bright colours and a sweet smell, but there are exceptions.

▲ A rafflesia flower opens out on the forest floor in Sumatra, Indonesia.

Largest flower

The largest flower in the world is the rafflesia parasite, which lives in the rainforests of Borneo and Sumatra. The plant actually lives inside the roots of a vine. At certain times of the year a lump grows out of the vine root and for several weeks gets bigger and bigger.

Eventually five leaves unfold, revealing a huge, orange, leathery flower which can be over 91 cm in diameter. The flower smells of rotting meat, and attracts small flies which pollinate it. After three or four days the flower collapses and disappears, leaving behind a small, woody fruit.

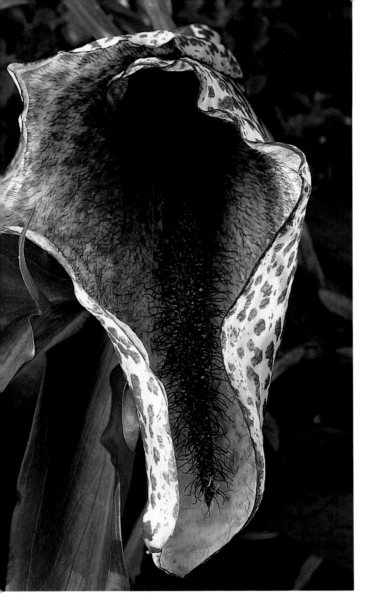

▲ The vile-smelling flower of the dead horse arum attracts blowflies, which help it to pollinate.

Fastest-growing flower

The titan arum is another giant flower from Sumatra. This flower grows at enormous speed, pushing upwards at the rate of about 10 cm a day. The final flower stands about 3 m tall, but only lasts for two days. Each plant only flowers about three times during its 20-year lifespan.

Nastiest flower

The dead horse arum grows on the islands of Corsica and Sardinia in the Mediterranean. Its appearance and smell must make it one of the nastiest flowers around. It grows near colonies of gulls, and produces its one flower at the height of the birds' breeding season. The flower is greyish-purple, streaked with pink, and about 25 cm across. It looks and smells like a piece of rotting flesh.

A gull colony is full of blowflies that are attracted by the broken and rotting eggs. The blowflies crawl into the centre of the arum flower to search for the source of the smell. In this way they pollinate the flower.

key facts

- The largest flower in the world is the rafflesia.
- The titan arum is the fastest-growing flower.
- Some flowers smell of rotting meat to attract pollinators.

Plants and people

People need plants. We could not live without the food they provide, the oxygen they create or the numerous other things we obtain from them and use to make our lives better.

Food

All humans and animals rely on plants for food. Most of the things we eat come from plants. Large areas of the world are farmed to produce crops to feed people or animals.

On the prairies of North America farmers grow grain crops such as wheat, maize and barley. In Asia rice is the **staple** grain crop. Tropical areas that have lots of sun and rain yield fruits such as bananas, pineapples, mangoes and papaya.

▼ In southeast Asia rice is grown in flooded fields called paddies and is the staple food for millions of people.

▲ Timber is one of the most useful plant products. Wood can be used to build houses and make furniture, or burnt for cooking and to provide warmth.

Wood

Trees provide us with wood, which has many uses. Wood is strong and light. It can be cut easily and can also be carved. Wood is very valuable for building, and is the most popular material for making furniture.

◄ The drug digitalis, used to treat heart disease comes from a flower, the foxglove.

Fuel

Plants provide us with fuel. In many areas of the world, people use wood for cooking and to provide heat.

The fossil fuels of coal, oil and natural gas are all formed from the remains of prehistoric plants and animals. They are extracted from the ground and burned in power stations to generate electricity.

Paper

Paper is made from wood. Each person uses one tree's worth of paper every year. Rubber and cork also come from trees. Cork is the thick, spongy bark of the cork oak tree, and rubber comes from the **sap** that is collected from rubber trees.

Textiles

Many of the materials we use for making clothes come from plants. Cotton is the most commonly used **natural fibre**. It is made from the cotton plant, and it is used for bed sheets, curtains, clothes, tablecloths, towels and many other purposes.

Medicines

For thousands of years people have known about the medicinal qualities of certain plants. A 60,000-year-old burial site in Iraq was found to contain the remains of eight different medicinal plants. Although many medicines today are made from chemicals, plant remedies still remain a valuable source of drugs.

key facts

- Without plants we could not survive.

- Plants provide us with food, fuel and building materials.

- Many plants have important medicinal qualities.

Glossary

Adaptation The way in which animals and plants change over many generations to survive better in their particular environment.

Cancer A disease that affects cells in the body, causing tumours to grow. Many people die of cancer each year.

Catkins The primitive flowers of some wind-pollinated trees.

Chlorophyll The green pigment found in plant leaves which absorbs light during the process of photosynthesis.

Coniferous A type of plant that produces seeds inside cones instead of flowers.

Deciduous Trees that shed their leaves in autumn.

Digestive juices The juices produced by an insect-eating plant that break down food into substances that can be absorbed and used by the plant.

Dormant Something that is not growing or being active.

Fertilization The joining together of the male and female cells to make a new plant.

Minerals Naturally occurring substances that are found in the ground. Minerals are needed for plants and animals to grow healthily.

Natural fibres Materials that occur naturally on the Earth – usually obtained from plants or animals.

Nutrients Substances that help animals and plants grow better.

Photosynthesis The method by which plants make food from sunlight, water and carbon dioxide.

Sap The watery liquid in plants.

Species A group of plants or animals that look alike and can breed with each other successfully.

Staple Main, or basic part of something.

Stomata The tiny openings in a leaf through which gases and water vapour pass.

Tropical Describes the part of the world between the Tropic of Cancer and the Tropic of Capricorn.

Water vapour Water in the form of a gas.

Further information

Books

Flowers, fruits and seeds,
Angela Royston,
Heinemann, 2000

Flowering plants,
Chris Oxlade,
Franklin Watts, 1998

Plants and flowers,
Sally Hewitt,
Watts, 1998

Websites

Biology4Kids.com
Angiosperms and Flowering Plants – read up on
these flowering plants and find out what dicots
and monocots are!
http://www.biology4kids.com/files/
plants_angiosperm.html

Conservation Breeding Specialist Group
This groups helps protect threatened plants and
animals. Explore the global zoo directory.
http://www.cbsg.org/

Paignton Zoo Environmental Park
A unique zoo that is home to some of the
world's most endangered plants and animals.
Lots of great pictures and fascinating facts.
http://www.rhads.net/zoo2001/

Angiosperms
Learn about these flowering plants that make up
the largest group in the plant kingdom.
http://pittsford.monroe.edu/jefferson/
calfieri/plants/Angiosperm.html

Places to Visit

UK
The Natural History Museum
Cromwell Road, London SW7 5BD

Oxford Museum of Natural History
Parks Road, Oxford OX1 3PW

Royal Museum
Chambers Street, Edinburgh EH1 1JF

Royal Botanic Gardens
Kew, Richmond, Surrey TW9 3AB

Australia
Australian Museum
6 College Street, Sydney NSW 2010

New Zealand
Canterbury Museum
Christchurch Botanic Gardens, Christchurch

Index